PARKINSON'S LAW

Master time management
and increase productivity

Written by Pierre Pichère
In collaboration with Brigitte Feys
Translated by Carly Probert

Business 50MINUTES.com

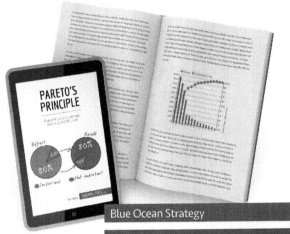

PARKINSON'S LAW   1

Key information
Introduction

THEORY   3

LIMITATIONS AND EXTENSIONS   8

Limitations and criticisms
Related models and extensions

PRACTICAL APPLICATION   13

Advice and top tips

CASE STUDY: THE BELGIAN CIVIL SERVICE   19

The modernisation of public services
Federalisation eventually proves Parkinson's theory

SUMMARY   23

FURTHER READING   25

PARKINSON'S LAW

KEY INFORMATION

- **Name:** Parkinson's Law.
- **Uses:** public management, administration, public services, human resource management.
- **Why is it successful?** It is a humorous, but very compelling, theory on the propensity of administration to grow, regardless of the amount of work required.
- **Key words:** civil servant, administration, working time, public management, bureaucracy.

INTRODUCTION

Shattering traditional ideas of working time, Parkinson's Law humorously emphasises the functioning of bureaucratic administration in the second half of the 20th century.

Full of British humour, and from a period when the perverse effects of the bureaucracy were being condemned (think of the famous novel *1984* by George Orwell, published in 1949), Cyril Northcote Parkinson (1909-1993), a British historian, published an article presenting Parkinson's Law in 1955. The law states that amount of civil service staff grows at a given rate (produced by an imaginative mathematical formula), regardless of the amount of work there is to do.

DEFINITION OF THE CONCEPT

Parkinson's Law is based on three statements:

- a person with a job to do will use all of the time available to finish it;
- employees always prefer to have a subordinate rather than a rival;
- employees mutually create work.

These three statements explain the natural tendency to increase the number of staff members. Although it is largely humorous, Parkinson's Law has the advantage of intelligibly explaining the development of bureaucracy.

THEORY

The State provides tasks for public powers (justice, police, diplomacy, etc.). In addition to this historical function, throughout the 20th century, social benefits have been developed to provide education, healthcare, health coverage and pensions. Although this second dimension operates differently from one nation to another, it can be found everywhere throughout Europe known as the 'welfare state'.

To run this vast operation, agents, called civil servants, are required. In France, for example, this refers to members of the three civil services (State, hospital and territorial), but more generally it refers, in a non-legal sense, to public officials. This nuance is needed to understand the scope of Parkinson's Law, created by a British author, as the term 'civil servant' is understood differently in other countries.

STAFF OF THE THREE CIVIL SERVICES IN FRANCE

In 2013, France employed 2.3 million civil servants, 1.14 million hospital officials and 1.8 million territorial officials, making a total of 5.24 million people. These figures include the owners and contractors.

By adopting an economic approach, we must also include the employees of publicly-funded private structures for public services. The total then amounts to approximately 6 million people, which accounts for roughly 25% of salaried employment in France.

Instinctively, reason dictates that public authorities hire agents for the tasks that it intends to entrust upon them. Logically, increasing the number of staff should correspond to an increase in the scope of action of the public authority in question. Parkinson's Law was created to counter this idea.

In the article he published in 1955 in the renowned magazine *The Economist*, Cyril Northcote Parkinson constructed the exact opposite reasoning. According to him, the increase in the number of civil servants is around 5.7% each year, regardless of the amount of work given to staff members.

Parkinson's argument alternates between serious data and an evident desire to amuse the reader. In the preface written for the French edition of a book on Parkinson's Law, published in the early 1980s, the great economist and demographer Alfred Sauvy (1898-1990) also cites Raymond Devos (French humourist, 1922-2006) and Jacques Tati (French scriptwriter and actor, 1907-1982) more willingly than the British classical economists Adam Smith (1723-1790) and David Ricardo (1772-1823) and he ranks Parkinson among the greatest fantasists of the time. However, this fantasy is more of a demonstration of British humour rather than a conclusion itself, and has become a classic reference in public management.

As a starting point to his reasoning, Cyril Northcote Parkinson points out that the more time an individual has to perform a task, the longer the task will take him to complete. He illustrates this with the example of an elderly woman and a young man who must each send a postcard.

Choosing the card, writing the text, stamping the card and mailing the card: all of these operations will certainly take a whole day for the person who has nothing else to do with their day, even though the task will not take more than half an hour for a very busy person. Therefore, there is no correlation between the amount of work required and the personnel chosen to carry out the work: this is the efficiency principle.

Parkinson's Law is based on two other statements:

- **State employees always prefer to have a subordinate rather than a rival.** This statement is demonstrated in Parkinson's article. If a civil servant believes – rightly or wrongly – that he has too much work, there are three options available:
  - leave the position;
  - request that another employee is hired;
  - ask for a subordinate.

  For reasons related to his career and potential promotions, he will prefer a subordinate rather than a colleague who would be considered a rival. Also, to ensure that a rivalry does not arise between him and his subordinate, he will prefer to hire two subordinates. The same problem will arise a few years later with both of these new recruits, so that in a short time five people will work there, instead of the one single person who worked there shortly before.
- **Civil servants mutually create work.** The increase in staff leads to heavier bureaucratic procedures, later

justifying the decision to hire. If the employee has a lot of work after recruiting two subordinates, he must have been overwhelmed beforehand. But, according to Parkinson, a significant portion of his workload comes from his new recruits, as there are now many more stages of validation.

From these two trends, Parkinson formed the law to which he gave his name, and which he expresses in a mathematical formula:

Parkinson's Law

$$x = \frac{(2k^m + l)}{n}$$

- *k* represents the number of employees seeking advancement by appointing subordinates to help them;
- *l* represents the difference between the age of appointment and the retirement age;
- *m* represents the number of hours devoted to answering memos within the department;
- *n* represents the number of new employees required each year.

To find the growth rate, the product is multiplied by 100 before being divided by the total for the previous year (noted *yn*), which gives:

Growth rate

$$\frac{100\,(2k^m + l)}{yn}\,\%$$

Parkinson's Law states that this rate is between 5.17% and 6.56%, irrespective of any variation in the amount of work involved.

LIMITATIONS AND EXTENSIONS

What is the scope of Parkinson's Law? The theory's scientific appearance accentuates its provocative nature. However, although it is intended to be humorous, it is still used in reflections on bureaucracy and its negative effects.

LIMITATIONS AND CRITICISMS

Quantification and growth rate

The methodological weakness of the law created by Parkinson is easy to identify, since most of the values of the equation cannot be determined. How can we actually quantify civil servants seeking promotions? This would require a mind-reading tool, which the State does not quite have yet. Similarly, measuring the number of hours spent answering memos is a nice thought, but it would mean sorting between useful and productive responses and those that the civil service could do without.

The result of the equation, a growth rate between 5.17% and 6.56%, should therefore not be taken at face value. In an article published around 20 years after introducing his law, Parkinson tried to show that it worked. Studying the staff of the British civil service, he himself acknowledged the weakness of the statistical basis on which he had constructed his reasoning. He nevertheless concluded the validity of the law by analysing the staff members of some British authorities, particularly the Ministry of Defence. However, this article once again had a strong satirical dimension, encouraging people to laugh about it.

We should therefore retain above all the logic of Parkinson's Law, without focusing too much on the mathematical formula, whose intention is probably more humorous than scientific. Therefore, let us look at the main things we can learn from Parkinson:

- The execution time for a task tends to reach the actual time available to complete the work.
- In a bureaucratic system, the workforce tends to grow rapidly, due to the advancement strategies of current employees, but also due to the higher number of procedures that justify the increase in the number of people linked to a task. This push towards increasing the number of civil servants leads to an economic impasse. In fact, these positions are funded by compulsory direct debits, which therefore follow an upward trend, reaching a threshold that suffocates the economic system.

Inapplicability to the company and management unfamiliarity

Parkinson's Law could not be applied to a company following constraints of productivity and increasing employment variation. On the contrary, this company will tend to reduce its workforce rather than increase it. Although in reality, Parkinson's Law does not correspond to techniques in management and human resources. These techniques work to motivate teams in order to increase productivity and therefore fight against the tendency to increase the time needed to complete a specific task.

RELATED MODELS AND EXTENSIONS

Parkinson's Law is still famous today. We can therefore approach other laws or principles which, for some, use up to date terminology and whose assumptions call upon those made by Parkinson.

- In 1970, **Laurence J. Peter** (Canadian educator, born in 1941) formulated the principle to which he gave his name, the Peter Principle. When competent employees are promoted to a higher position, there will always come a time when the positions in a company (especially at management level) are staffed by incompetent employees. This principle is similar to Parkinson's Law in that it relates to the promotion of civil servants.
- In 1975, **Frederick Brooks** (computer engineer and university professor, born in 1931) published a book entitled *The Mythical Man-Month*. He explains how adding staff to a project that is already delayed will only increase the final delay. He criticises the unit of measurement frequently used in project management, that of man-months, i.e. the amount of work performed by a person in one month. However, this volume is largely dependent on the general organisation of the project, working conditions, etc. This conclusion has common ground with the explanation of Parkinson on the expansion of work to fill the amount of time available to complete it. This approach has also been compared to some of the laws on the expansion of gases, but this parallel is more of a comparison than a similarity.
- Considering Parkinson as a writer on something between

humour and economics, it is also possible to compare him to **Auguste Detoeuf** (industrialist and writer, 1883-1947). He was the author of several collections of sayings and thoughts and had studied at the École Polytechnique, then going on to found the company *Alsthom*. His texts are full of reflections from the business world, with several references to time and how best to use it. These humorous thoughts are often similar to the approach of Parkinson's Law on the expansion of the time necessary to accomplish a specific task.

In the world of social sciences, since the early 20th century, several authors have studied the effects of bureaucracy, releasing findings that are similar to those established by Cyril Northcote Parkinson. Three of them are worth mentioning here.

- According to **Max Weber** (German sociologist, 1864-1920), the rise of capitalism leads to a new type of authority. While feudal societies relying on personal authority and despotic regimes (such as Bonapartism) are based on charismatic authority, capitalism generates obedience to the rule, so-called rational authority. A person has control according to the position they occupy in the hierarchy and the powers that are associated with that position. The term 'bureaucracy' then appeared, used by Max Weber, without pejorative connotations, to describe the growing role of state administration and companies in modern societies. Conversely, he considers bureaucracy to be the most successful social form, as it is based on rule of the law and helps those involved in the

tasks to survive.
- The approach of **Ludwig van Mises** (Austrian-American economist, 1881-1973) is much more critical. In 1944 he denounced, in *The Bureaucracy*, the increasing weight of public administrations in contemporary economies and the obstacle that they represent for the growth of economic activity. This text may have inspired Parkinson who, claiming to have developed a rule explaining the growth rate in the number of civil servants, was concerned about a time when this category would represent the entire workforce.
- Throughout these investigations, French sociologist **Michel Crozier** (1922-2013) demonstrated how the officials in a bureaucratic system gradually free themselves from the rules to develop room for freedom. This research may explain why employees of large organisations would take more and more time to complete their work, thus establishing the conditions for hiring new agents, as described by Parkinson.

Since the 1970s, the theory of new public management has been concerned with the management of public administration, seeking methods of modernisation largely inspired by the management of private companies. Treating users as customers requires the development of efficient agencies that distribute services, as the central government merely sets the guidelines. This approach, widely accepted but also often criticised, tries to overcome bureaucracy and its peculiarities.

PRACTICAL APPLICATION

Whether in large private companies or public administrations, managers are trying to establish tools to battle the underlying trends identified by Parkinson.

However, in public administration these means are often more limited than in the private sector. Staff regulations limit the hierarchical powers: they can only be fired in exceptional circumstances, and the definition of wages rarely takes into account the objective elements of performance. In all Western countries, recent developments have led to an improvement in the efficiency of public administration, with the following aims:

- more closely controlling officials and thus limiting the working time expansion effect;
- simplifying administrative procedures by countering bureaucratic trends;
- finally, limiting the growth of the workforce in public services, including seeking to reduce the number of civil servants, going against Parkinson's predictions about the inevitable increase in the number of state officials at a given speed.

ADVICE AND TOP TIPS

Managing objectives

Many countries have implemented management by objectives. Until the early 1990s, national budgets rarely included the link between objectives and means. In most OECD

(Organization for Economic Cooperation and Development) Member States, these procedures were then developed gradually. In France, for example, the organic law relating to the finance laws (LOLF), adopted in 2001 and enforced in 2006, is part of this movement. It plans national budgets by programme, with strengthened capacity to check their performance. It is therefore designed to allocate resources to achieve the objectives set by the public authorities, under the watchful eye of Parliament. These new procedures tend to better organise the work of the civil service and its employees, and therefore to fight against the negative effects of bureaucracy as analysed by Parkinson. It is necessary to determine a limited number of clear objectives so that they do not contradict each other.

Developing incentives and checks

Supporting this management by objectives on a national level, the involvement of public officials has been the subject of many experiments. Encouraging workers to be more efficient and enhancing checks are two sides to the same question: how can the productivity of public services be improved?

Denmark, for example, has developed a system of contractual remuneration for public officials, with the aim that the share of performance-related pay will reach 20% of the salary. This assessment is carried out through a dialogue between the employee and the supervisor, overseen by a union representative. A recent reassessment of this policy that was established 20 years ago shows greater acceptance of the performance objectives when part of the salary depends on them, since the employee understands and appropriates the indicators and evaluation methods. Other countries have chosen to develop the salaries of public managers, those who manage services and agencies, and who receive bonuses or promotions based on the success of their teams.

There is still a need to develop relevant performance indicators. They must match public service objectives, without being purely countable. It would be difficult to measure the performance of a police officer based on the number of tickets issued or arrests. But how can his work in crime prevention be evaluated? How can we measure events that did not happen? Furthermore, in all sectors, private or public, any assessment involves a risk of misappropriation by those subject to it. The participants will adopt attitudes likely to improve the indicators, to the detriment of other aspects of their work that are equally essential but less easily measured by indicators. Establishing performance measures, to gradually control performance according to set objectives, calls for prudence and careful consideration.

Finally, incentives and checks can be made more difficult by the status of public service. In countries with career systems, the immovability of civil servants appointed to statutory positions can hamper the establishment of a true structure of individual and collective incentives.

CAREER SYSTEMS AND POSITION SYSTEMS

There are two types of organisation in public services.

- In career systems, employees join the civil service following an exam or competition. They are subject to a hierarchical organisation, where progress is linked to the points obtained from seniority and grading. Job security is generally guaranteed.
- Conversely, position systems call for a person who is thought to be most qualified for a function, even if it does not belong to public services. More flexible, this system is closer to the private labour market.

Note that in France, the two systems coexist. The civil service falls within the career system, while local councils function more like the private labour market, with officials but also with employees from outside to fill some positions on a temporary contract.

Downsizing

Parkinson's Law was created in the 1950s, a period of strong growth in relatively closed economies, where neither the weight of public spending nor the competition between tax systems were yet a cause for debate. The situation has since changed. Public budgets, particularly since the 2008 financial crisis, have been tightened; European states want to control spending. Significant stabilisation measures, even reductions in the public workforce, were initiated from the early 1990s. OECD figures suggest a relative stability in the number of officials in most of the Member States of this organisation between 1991 and 2001. Only Luxembourg shows an average increase of 4% per year. France was not part of this investigation.

Several strategies have been implemented:

- Privatisations undertaken since the 1990s in many countries have led to a change of status for civil servants or those that are newly hired. This reduction of state intervention was observed in France, for example, with the privatisation of large companies like France Telecom. Officials from the Ministry of Post and Telecommunications were gradually replaced by private employees from the France Telecom company (now Orange), and the state now only holds a small share of the capital.
- Many countries have been trying for several years to contain the public workforce. Policies on the non-replacement of agents, retiring and hiring have led to stagnation, or even a slight decrease in the number of civil servants.
- Some states have more obviously contradicted Parkinson's Law, employing a more brutal policy of noticeable decline in the number of state officials. In Germany, in the 1990s, the state separated itself from some officials following the country's reunification.

Decentralisation policies created an illusion of significant decreases. Thus, according to data from the Court of Auditors, public officials remained stable in state public services between 2000 and 2007, a first for countries like

France, which is very attached to public intervention. But at the same time, the number of local council employees has grown by 400 000, as a result of successive measures of decentralisation that transferred new responsibilities to local authorities, including technical personnel in charge of colleges (general councils) and high schools (regional councils). It is therefore more of a waterbed operation than a real policy for the stabilisation of civil servants.

CASE STUDY: THE BELGIAN CIVIL SERVICE

Belgium is an interesting example of public service based on a rigid status, with considerable employees of approximately 840 000 people by the end of 2013. Recent reforms have attempted to reverse the trend of steady increase in enrolment described by Parkinson. It is a way of responding to the economic crisis, but also of bouncing back from the erosion of trust between the government and its citizens. While efforts have been made by the federal state, the progressive federalisation of the country led regions and communities to develop their staff to take on new tasks, so that the number of public employees has continued to grow.

THE MODERNISATION OF PUBLIC SERVICES

Traditionally, the Belgian civil service was characterised by a low mobility of employees, a considerable career system and a certain rigidity, like many European public services. From the 1990s, the increasing burden of public debt, which peaked at 137% of GDP in 1993, led the country to try to modernise public services to keep costs down while improving efficiency. Public services account for about 17% of Belgian GDP, a relatively low rate, but hospital staff must be added to this, and they are not included in the statistical basis.

At the federal level, management training programmes, career mobility and leadership accountability were introduced to increase efficiency and fight against the excessive increase in working time and in numbers of public officials as described by Parkinson. Regions and communities also evolved their methods. In Flanders, six-year terms were introduced for senior officials. The civil service was reorganised into departments, with large delegations to managers. In Wallonia, regrouping has taken place and the regional authority has further divided the operational functions between the various departments.

> **DID YOU KNOW?**
>
> The Belgian civil service often uses contract staff, temp workers or subcontractors to perform specific tasks, despite their higher cost, in order to decrease the rigidity of public administration. In fact, these contributors are more flexible because they are not appointed.
>
> To become civil servants, candidates must pass a series of exams, while for the selection of senior officials, in addition to this first selection, candidates must meet with a disciplinary board composed of specialists in the skills required for the vacancies, who are generally professionals from the public and private sectors.

FEDERALISATION EVENTUALLY PROVES PARKINSON'S THEORY

The federal government has also committed to a policy of reducing staff in the Belgian public services. In the country's budgetary commitments, actions are taken to respect the

European Stability and Growth Pact, leading to significant savings in staff expenses listed for the years 2010 to 2014. They exceed the 300 million euros listed for 2013 and 2014.

At the same time, the country increased its federalisation, transferring many responsibilities to local and regional authorities. Efforts to contain public employment at the deferral level have been thwarted by the rise of civil services in regions and communities. Employment in the federal sector increased moderately between 2000 and 2010, by 4.5% in total (far from the 5-6% per year anticipated by Parkinson). However, over the same period, it increased by 20.5% in communities and provinces and 22.7% in regions. Employment in the public sector across all levels grew faster than total employment between 2000 and 2010 (13.8% against 9.2%). The uncertainty of the private market is off-putting to candidates who are searching for job security, ensuring stability in their career and their tasks.

This example illustrates the difficulties faced by countries when containing the number of public officials. The legacy of previous legislation that new managerial practices struggle to soften, the legitimate expectations of the population on public services and the decentralisation or federalisation movement which is very pronounced in Belgium, but present in many European countries where the local level is valued, all lead to difficult control over staff – not to mention that this weapon can be used to fight against unemployment. But at a time when public accounts are closely scrutinised by the European Commission, the Court of Auditors and financial markets, and where globalisation exerts a downward pressure on the level of compulsory taxes by creating competition between fiscal systems in Western nations, this issue appears in the political and economic agenda. All states are trying to limit the predictions of Parkinson, with relative success.

SUMMARY

- Parkinson's Law predicts a proportionate annual increase in the number of civil servants of between 5.17% and 6.56%, regardless of the workload.
- Cyril Northcote Parkinson bases his reasoning on three assumptions:
  - a state employee will use all of the time available to complete his work;
  - he will always prefer to have subordinates rather than co-workers, based on the logic of career advancement;
  - civil servants create work for each other.
- Parkinson's Law is highly satirical, but agrees with more scientific theories on bureaucracy.
- It draws the reader's attention to a major financial challenge, but seems to completely neglect the aspect of human resource management and efficiency.
- Today, public services are making considerable efforts, especially in human resources, to fight against their natural tendency to grow, in order to control public finances and the quality of the services delivered to the population.

We want to hear from you!
Leave a comment on your online library
and share your favourite books on social media!

FURTHER READING

BIBLIOGRAPHY

- Demonty, B. (2013) Record de fonctionnaires en Belgique. *Le Soir*. [Online]. [Accessed 7 July 2014]. Available from: <http://www.lesoir.be/160948/article/actualite/belgique/2013-01-14/record-fonctionnaires-en-belgique>
- OECD. (2005) *Modernising Government: The Way Forward*. [Online]. [Accessed 7 July 2014]. Available from: <http://www.oecd-ilibrary.org/governance/modernising-government_9789264010505-en>
- OECD. (2007) *Examen de l'OCDE sur la gestion des ressources humaines dans la fonction publique : Belgique*. [Online]. [Accessed 7 July 2014]. Available from: <http://www.oecd.org/fr/gouvernance/emploi-public/39375860.pdf>
- OECD. (2011) *Preésentation de l'Étude économique sur la Belgique 2011 : Trois enjeux stratégiques pour la Belgique*. [Online]. [Accessed 7 July 2014]. Available from: <http://www.oecd.org/fr/belgique/etudeeconomiquedelabelgique2011.htm>
- Parkinson, C. N. (1983) *Parkinson's Laws*. Paris: Robert Laffont.

© 50MINUTES.com, 2016. All rights reserved.

www.50minutes.com

Ebook EAN: 9782806266217

Paperback EAN: 9782806270047

Legal Deposit: D/2015/12603/428

Cover: © Primento

Digital conception by Primento, the digital partner of publishers.

Printed in Poland
by Amazon Fulfillment
Poland Sp. z o.o., Wrocław